BLESSINGS,
BLESSINGS,
AND MORE
BLESSINGS,

+ **OBEDIENCE**

'2003'

OBEDIENCE

The Key to God's Divine Favor

Obedience
The Key to God's Divine Favor

ISBN 1-889389-05-6

Note: In some Scripture quotations, italics have been added by the author for emphasis only.

See us at http://www.endtimewave.com

TABLE OF CONTENTS

DEDICATION

To my darling wife, Patti who is the essence of love, a personal source of encouragement and inspiration.

To my daughters, Kristen and Tiffany who continually provide love and support for my leadership potential.

To the Christian Provision Ministries Family and friends, for their support, love and commitment to the publication of this book.

May the peace, promise and prosperity of our Lord be your portion.

FOREWORD

Bishop Charles Mellette has struck a chord in the topic chosen within these pages. Obedience is a subject many times overlooked in the Church. Obedience becomes more than just a passive way of behavior for an individual. The Bible teaches us that obedience is actually an offensive weapon to destroy the spirit of disobedience.

I believe that this book will challenge you in several areas. One area will be in the way obedience produces power in the life of the believer. Another way is that obedience puts us in right standing with our God.

Rightfully so, this book exposes the attack of the enemy in the area of our obedience. We must guard our commitment to be obedient with all diligence. This book also brings our attention to the fact that it is in the wilderness times of our lives, when our obedience is tested the most. We find that it is in our "desert" season, when God decides to allow tests and trials to become a handy tool to evaluate our level of commitment, and obedience to Him and His Word.

After reading this book, I was more confident than ever about one thing; when hanging out with God, my obedience is far greater than any sacrifice I could conjure up.

The favor I receive in God or in believing God is in direct proportion to my level of obedience. I agree with my brother and friend, Bishop Charles Mellette in saying that obedience is the "Key to God's Divine Favor."

I am so grateful to God for allowing this powerful book to be released to the Body of Christ at such a critical time as this. I am trusting the Spirit of the Lord to use this material to bless you and change your mind set. It is a must read book for everyone in the Body of Christ. I encourage everyone that reads this book to recommend it to other fellow believers; for it is surely God-ordained.

Apostle John Tetsola
Senior Minister
Ecclesia Word Ministries International
Bronx, New York

INTRODUCTION

There is power in obedience. As you read this book, expect to receive the power that obedience produces! Expect to see your faith increase! Expect to have your mind renewed! This book will provide a greater depth of understanding on a subject we talk a lot about but really lack a clear understanding.

Most Christians recognize that the devil does exist. If you believe that God exists, then you have to believe that the devil also exists. If you believe in good, then you also must believe in evil. It's that simple. Make no mistake about it; the devil is as real as can be. The Word of God clearly states that the devil's mission is to steal, kill and destroy. He's a vicious opponent of the kingdom of God and his sole purpose in life is to make your life miserable. In fact, if he could, he would kill us all!

If someone wanted to kill you, what would you do? Most probably, you'd make sure your defenses were always up. In other words, you'd watch your back. However, when it comes to Satan, most of us have our backsides exposed. While we acknowledge that he's our enemy, while we preach against him, while we sing about him and while we testify about him, we do not wage an accurate assault against him. This is mostly because we are still unaware of how to actively defuse his tactics in our lives.

God has called us to an abundant life. He has decreed victory, victory, victory! Anything else is a shadow of the life that God has purposed and planned for you. Have you been leading a defeated life? Are you living in victory, or are you constantly "going through" and asking God "Why?" If so, there's an answer for you!

You don't have to take the devil's junk! You can be liberated from all of his tactics and attacks upon your life if you would just learn to walk in obedience to God and His established laws. Obedience is the key to unlock the door called victory. It paves the path to a power-charged life in which you are the head and not the tail. Your obedience serves notice to the rest of the world that you have determined that Jesus Christ is the Lord of your life, and that determination will allow you to walk in harmony with God. You must stare in the eyes of disobedience and be willing to revenge it. You must be willing to sense that attack in your life against your obedience and faithfulness to God and declare an all out war upon it. Then, the key to the victory is that your weaponry be clothed in obedience to the heavenly vision that has been given to you by God!

Bishop Charles Mellette
January 1997

CHAPTER I

OBEDIENCE - THE DEATH OF THE SERPENT

Behold, to obey is better than sacrifice, and to hearken than the fat of rams.

I Samuel 15:22b

What is obedience? For the Christian, obedience is not an option but a mandate from God. Obedience is defined as "the act or instance of obeying," "the quality or state of being obedient within a sphere of jurisdiction," and "being submissive to the constraint or the command of authority issued." Obedience is an inward condition of the heart that is reflected in the words we speak and the deeds we do. God has instituted boundaries to guide our actions. As long as we operate within these boundaries, we will align ourselves in a place of safety and protection and will discover that everything has a way of working itself out. As we walk in obedience, we are covered by the umbrella of God's protective arm and His never-ending provision. It's only when

1

we operate outside of these boundaries do we begin to succumb to problems.

A good illustration of this is that a river or a stream does fine as long as it's flowing within its banks. The waters are well controlled and any life forms that come in contact with that river or stream suffer no harm. We even enjoy the experiences of these rivers and streams; they're good for fishing and swimming. We love to picnic and enjoy the beauty of these waters. Although the waters ebb and flow within inches of us, we do not fear. But when a river swells and begins to surge beyond its boundary, people's lives are threatened because the nature of the river has been altered. When the water reaches for a course beyond that which was established for it by God, its nature changes from productive to destructive. The once comforting presence of the water is replaced by a life-threatening force. The river has now become a devastating flood. Its beauty is obscured by the magnitude of death and destruction it causes in its path. The water is running outside of its given jurisdiction, and its natural order of peace and harmony is disturbed. While once people flocked to the beauty of the river, now they are running away in fear and terror.

When we are disobedient to God, we are exactly like that river. We go beyond our boundaries, and our nature changes. We become carriers of death and destruction. While we once were a blessing and a source of life to those around us, we now become a channel of death and decay. As we reap what we have sown, others are negatively impacted by our disobedience. The devil gains footing upon the disobedience in our lives, for that is the place he will utilize to bring devastation to us. This is why God talks to us about the importance of obedience. He wants to curb our appetites from things that desire to consume us.

However, there is more to obedience than that. God is not some "cosmic kill-joy" just waiting to stop us from enjoying what appears to be the pleasures of life. No! He wants to direct us into paths of righteousness for His Name's sake, because in those paths, He can give us the desires of our hearts.

And it shall come to pass, if thou shalt hearken diligently unto the voice of the LORD thy God, to observe and to do all his commandments which I command thee this day, that the LORD thy God will set thee on high above all nations of the earth:

And all these blessings shall come on thee, and overtake thee, if thou shalt hearken unto the voice of the LORD thy God.

Blessed shalt thou be in the city, and blessed shalt thou be in the field.

Blessed shall be the fruit of thy body, and the fruit of thy ground, and the fruit of thy cattle, the increase of thy kine, and the flocks of thy sheep.

Blessed shall be thy basket and thy store.

3

Blessed shalt thou be when thou comest in, and blessed shalt thou be when thou goest out.

The LORD shall cause thine enemies that rise up against thee to be smitten before thy face: they shall come out against thee one way, and flee before thee seven ways.

The LORD shall command the blessing upon thee in thy storehouses, and in all that thou settest thine hand unto; and he shall bless thee in the land which the LORD thy God giveth thee.

The LORD shall establish thee an holy people unto himself, as he hath sworn unto thee, if thou shalt keep the commandments of the LORD thy God, and walk in his ways.

And all people of the earth shall see that thou art called by the name of the LORD; and they shall be afraid of thee.

And the LORD shall make thee plenteous in goods, in the fruit of thy body, and in the fruit of thy cattle, and in the fruit of thy ground, in the land which the LORD sware unto thy fathers to give thee.

The LORD shall open unto thee his good treasure, the heaven to give the rain unto thy land in his season, and to bless all the work of thine hand: and thou shalt lend unto many nations, and thou shalt not borrow.

And the LORD shall make thee the head, and not the tail; and thou shalt be above only, and thou shalt not be beneath; if that thou hearken unto the commandments of the LORD

**thy God, which I command thee this day, to observe and to
do them:**

Deuteronomy 28:1-13

God can pour out blessings in a proportion that we don't
have room enough to receive!! Taking a look at Deuteronomy
28, we see these are the things that God wants to manifest in
our lives. And it only takes one thing . . . your obedience!

AND WHEN THE SERPENT SPOKE

The serpent is a noxious snake. It is malignant in character
and intent. It is vicious, poisonous, evil and deadly! Unless
you know what you're doing, don't mess with a snake! Don't
even touch it! One touch is all that is needed to send you
from the heights of life, to the portals of death. A snake's
nature is to steal life from any creature that comes in its
path....including mankind. Because of its character and
repulsiveness, it is also referred to as "a devil" and also
defined as "a treacherous person." The snake itself is not the
devil. A lot of people have built their theology on the fact that
the snake is the devil. That's absurd! A lot of people may
have thought that the snake in the Garden of Eden was
actually the devil, but the snake was actually an innocent
creature fulfilling its purpose on the earth until the spirit of
the devil chose to dwell within it.

The devil needs a life form -- any form -- in which to operate in the earth. In the case of the Garden of Eden he chose the snake, although he could have chosen any animal he wanted to. When Lucifer, God's chief angel, was kicked out of Heaven and placed in the earth, he landed here in the form of a spirit. Unless it found a body, he, a spirit could not operate -- legally -- in the earth. The spirit of the devil decided to live in the serpent. He could have picked a cow, a chicken, a hippo, or anything else. But the devil just happened to pick the serpent. That's why, from the beginning of time up until this day, the serpent has been the representation of the devil. Satan's first recorded appearance on earth in the Scriptures is when he, as a serpent, deceived Eve in the Garden of Eden. This was man's first act of disobedience. This act created a door which allowed the entrance of the enemy into the lives of God's created ones.

The inhabitation of the snake by the devil immediately changed its nature. The enemy overpowered the animal's nature and it became a mirror image of the devil and the devil's nature. The same happens when we willfully disobey God; we begin to reflect the enemy's nature. People are innocent until they allow the spirit of the devil to inhabit them. The spirit of the devil will take control of your thoughts and your actions. If the Spirit of God is permitted to live inside of you, you will be controlled by the Spirit of God. Which ever spirit you permit to reside within you will be the spirit that will take control of your life. And you'll look, sound, and act like that spirit. People will know what spirit is dwelling in you, for there will be a scent, a word, a performance that will clearly state "I am from the kingdom of ..."

God and the devil are both spirits that need bodies to inhabit in order to operate in the earth. That's why God wants you to be saved....by inhabiting you, He can reach other people and minister life through you! And, conversely, that's why the devil wants you to live for him, because he can reach other people and destroy their lives through you!

When you live a life that is obedient to God, the devil won't have any place in you or with you. Disobedience is the very thing that gives life to the devil. It is the life support system of evil. When God is allowed to live in us, the devil is eliminated from our presence!

AND GOD SAID...AND GOD SAW

God said, let us make man in our image, after our likeness and let them have dominion over the fish of the sea, over the fowl of the air and over the cattle and over all the earth and over every creeping thing that creepeth upon the earth.

So God created man in His own image and the image of God created He him male and female created He them.

Genesis 1:26-27

God spoke to Himself when He decided to create man. He did not consult any of His created beings on heaven or on earth. He made us as He is and called us out of Him. We did not come from someone's animal like the theory of evolution says. When God desired us He said, "Let us make man." He reached within Himself, opened His mouth, spoke and began to call us out of His very Being. We came forth with purpose because we came out of God. We are as He is. We were made in His Image. What is God? God is a Creator...a Consuming Fire...a Dominator...a Giver...Omnipotent....All Powerful.... Omnipresent... Always Present.....a Producer...a Comforter...an Initiator. God is all that and then some! He's an awesome God! So, we should be the same, since we're born of Him and made in His Image!! We must not limit or shortchange ourselves. We must become comfortable and walk in the Image of God!

God actually saw man being successful. He actually saw man giving honor, respect and obedience to Him before creation was completed. Therefore, since God's opinion of man has not changed, our purpose on the earth has not changed!! You are a winner! You are a victor!

God already sees the successful completion of everything that He has assigned and released us to do. He told the prophet Jeremiah, "For I know the thoughts that I think toward you, thoughts of peace, and not of evil, to give you an expected end." When He calls us to start a thing, He already sees the finished product! If God did not see us successfully completing what He called us to do, He would never have called us to start anything. That's why there are times that He's allowed us to look at our own lives, whether in a dream or a vision, and has given us a glimpse of where we are going. Sometimes, He may even show someone else or even a prophet a quick peek of our destination in life. He allows us to see what He wants to do with us, and then God backs us all the way to the back of the line and says, "OK, now start what I've allowed you to see."

The secret to your success is locked up in your obedience to God.

> **And God blessed them and God said to them, be fruitful and multiply and replenish the earth and subdue it and have dominion over the fish of the sea and over the fowl of the air and over every living thing that moveth upon the earth.**

> **And God said, Behold I have given you every herb bearing seed which is upon the face of all the earth and every tree in the which is the fruit of the tree yielding seed; to you it shall be for meat.**

> **And to every beast of the earth and to every fowl of the air and to everything that creepeth upon the earth wherein there is life, I have given every green herb for meat and it was so.**

And God saw everything that He had made and behold it was very good and the evening and the morning were the six day.

Genesis 1:28-31

At this point in creation, God had taken a look within Himself and had seen what He had made and what He intended to bring forth. He said that it was good and He hadn't even formed it yet! The Scriptures give us an account of how God saw us before we ever came into being. Just think....God already saw you being successful and obeying His Voice before your mother ever gave birth to you! He actually saw you as good ...even though He knew that man was going to fall....even though He knew that a sinful nature would arise within us. If God did not have intentions of greatness for your life, you would not be alive today! You could have been an undeveloped seed never coming to conception. Your mother could have aborted you. As you walked this life, there were many times you could have died. But, all of that escaped you! Why? Because God has destined that you would complete what He has called you to do!!

God has to awaken us to what it is He has called each of us to do, for most of us don't even have an inkling of our calling in life. We do things because we're seeking money or the approval of men. We allow others to choose our path for us because we don't allow God to direct our path.

OBEDIENCE -- THE DEATH OF THE SERPENT

A man's heart deviseth his way: but the LORD directeth his steps.

Proverbs 16:9

The steps of a good man are ordered by the LORD: and he delighteth in his way.

Psalms 37:23

He made you and brought you to this earth for a specific purpose, which is up to you to discover and then fulfill. As you walk in obedience to God, you will discover His purpose for your life. You will discover destiny. You will discover life.

When people don't understand, or when they are not conscious of their purpose, they begin to get involved with things that they ought not. They have no solid idea of God's real purpose for their life, and will follow the path of least resistance. They will take the lazy way through life and never realize or actualize their potential. Instead of becoming a neurosurgeon, a person might become a physician's assistant or a nurse's aide. Instead of becoming a concert pianist, a person may opt to become a music teacher. The list is endless, as are the possibilities of missing God when we are ignorant of His purposes for our lives.

The entrance of thy words giveth light; it giveth understanding unto the simple.

Psalms 119:130

Don't let situations or people try to dictate what you are, who you are and what you can't be and what you cannot do! Go to the Bible and get a revelation of who you are for yourself! See yourself in the Image of God; walk and live by that Image alone. Gain some understanding of whom God has said that you really are. There are too many people living their lives based upon what someone else has told them. What others say really has nothing to do with what God has already said concerning your life! Let God be true and every man a liar.

You cannot leave the destiny and the course of your life in the hands of somebody else. You have got to go to the Bible yourself and get a clearer understanding of what God has to say about you. Frankly, it doesn't matter what you have been through, and it doesn't matter how you have lived. All the hell you have overcome doesn't matter when you begin to understand what God has said about you. Besides which, only the spiritually dead are in hell. Only the spiritually dead should be living in an eternal state of dissatisfaction. You have been resurrected to a new life and new hope. Newness is all around you, so think on those things and they will manifest in your life.

OBEDIENCE -- THE DEATH OF THE SERPENT

Therefore if any man be in Christ, he is a new creature: old things are passed away; behold, all things are become new.

2 Corinthians 5:17

You can make a dramatic, sanctified, and glorious change for the better, but people will tend to remember you as you used to be. That's understandable, for they did the same to Jesus. A servant is not above his master. People will always have an "I knew you when.." mentality. It's up to you to move beyond the opinions of men. If you don't understand that what God says means more than what people say, you will always be bound by what folks think. When I understand what God has to say about me and my purpose, the hell that I've been through does not prevent me from walking in the glorious light of God! In fact, it can't, because darkness can not dwell with light. So, I am now free to walk as Jesus sees me, despite the past life that I once lived.

The Apostle Paul discovered this on the road to Damascus. Although others considered him unworthy to speak, teach and disciple others in the Name of Christ, his obedience to the call of salvation made him immediately worthy! It did not even matter what the original apostles thought, God was determined to get glory out of the life of Paul.

13

Brethren, I count not myself to have apprehended: but this one thing I do, forgetting those things which are behind, and reaching forth unto those things which are before,

Philippians 3:13

When you discover who and what you are in Him, your life will never be the same. He doesn't drag the darkness of your past into the light of your future. Now that the light is on, forget about the darkness! The darkness doesn't matter anymore! The brightness of the light in you totally obliterates the darkness. What I used to do, and what you used to be, what I used to experience, and what you've been in the past, is just matter that is shattered....it doesn't matter anymore. Why? Because what God has to say about us carries more weight than what any of us have to say about ourselves or about each other! Choose to hear what it is God has to say about you! If you want to live and get on with your life, I would recommend that you read the Bible and hear what God has to say about you. For every time that someone ripped your confidence and told you that you've never been or will be any good, God will speak hundreds of times and confirm your worth and your value through His Word. He will discharge every seed of negativity that has been planted within your spirit. The devil is the father of lies, and is the originator of every lie that comes against you. The devil inspires lots of lies: "You are no good and you'll never be any good " and "Nothing good ever came out of you and nothing good will ever come out of you." Most of us heard these lies at one time or another. And the fact is, if you believed the lie, you will be exactly what they say. If you knew someone was a "born liar" would you adhere to anything he said? Of course, not! You would tune out everything he is saying to and about you. Why? Because you know his word is not trustworthy. The same is true for the devil. The good news is that you don't have to believe that lie! Why? Because you mean something to God!

> **I will praise thee; for I am fearfully and wonderfully made: marvellous are thy works; and that my soul knoweth right well.**
>
> **Psalms 139:14**

The Bible says that you are created in His Image. He is the Manufacturer of your life. And, if God is the Manufacturer of your life, that means that God knows all about your life from the hairs on the top of your head to the soles of the bottom of your feet. God knows all about you. Why? Because He is your Maker. No one understands a product the way the Manufacturer does; and no one really understands the original intent, design and function of that product like the Manufacturer. God understands every facet of you because He manufactured you! Anytime you've got a problem with your body, no one can fix it quite like He can. Do you know why? Because nobody understands it like He does!

If I depend on you to fix me, I might get put together the wrong way. If I expect you to work something out for me, it might get worked out the wrong way. If I depend upon my Manufacturer, everything that needs to be fixed and worked out will be fixed and worked in His Divine order, and according to the original design and blueprints. He knows me. You can't make me stop lying and you can't make me stop cussing. You can't make me stop being abusive to people. You can't make me stop doing things that I ought not be doing...... but my Manufacturer can! Why? Because He knows which buttons to push to make me stop and go. You can't control my heart, but God can! You can't control my spirit....but God can! Our Maker has made us and showed us the Image in which we are to flow. I didn't always know how I was supposed to talk, but My Manufacturer has showed me and now I have learned how to talk. He showed me how I am supposed to carry myself and now I carry myself that way. Why? Because I have learned through the school of obedience.

God built us with His characteristics. We didn't come here like the devil; we learned to be like the devil. You learned how to do the things that you do. You were not born knowing how to get over on people and just "get by." You learned that in the course of life. No one was born knowing how to praise and give glory and honor to God. We had to learn how to do it.

Know ye that the LORD he is God: it is he that hath made us, and not we ourselves; we are his people, and the sheep of his pasture.

Psalms 100:3

The fact that God manufactured us is the only thing that distinguishes you and I from every other creature on the earth. Nothing else has that status. When God created everything else, He spoke it into existence. He called the mountains to appear from the ground and called oceans, lakes and rivers to appear from the waters. He called clouds and stars to appear in the air, but when He called us, He called us out of Himself. We didn't come out of the water. We didn't just happen to fall out of the sky. He didn't just call us to appear out of the woods, but He called us out of His innermost being. Maybe you don't know where you were born. Maybe you don't know your father or your mother. Maybe you don't know where you came from, but just know that you came out of God!! We have the power to think, to feel and to decide. We have the ability to make moral choices and the capacity to decide whether or not we are going to increase spiritually or decrease spiritually. God has given you the remarkable power of choice.

FOREVER BLESSED

So God created man in his own image, in the image of God created he him; male and female created he them.

17

And God blessed them, and God said unto them, Be fruitful, and multiply, and replenish the earth, and subdue it: and have dominion over the fish of the sea, and over the fowl of the air, and over every living thing that moveth upon the earth.

Genesis 1:27-28

When God speaks of man, He is also speaking about the woman because she was extracted from within the man. God blessed them and commanded them to forever be blessed. When He began to tell them about being fruitful and multiplying, He said, "From now on, you will be what I made you from the beginning". We're always supposed to be blessed. Don't get mad when you see someone walking in the blessings of God. Don't get an attitude because they have an appetite to be blessed! Get hungry! Don't get an attitude because someone has a mind for success! Renew your mind! Don't get an attitude because someone has a mind to increase! Dream big! God built us for multiplication and expansion; He told us to multiply and replenish. God never has drought on His mind, but an overflow of provision. We are supposed to be blessed. Don't get jealous because people around you are visibly blessed. Begin to increase yourself!

Isn't it amazing that God created each of us to be blessed, and commanded that we would be blessed forever, but then when some of us do what God made us to do, there are others that get an attitude? Do you know why they get an attitude? It's because our blessing threatens them when they don't know that they are supposed to blessed, too! When you don't acknowledge that others are supposed to be blessed, you'll have a problem when blessings show up in their life. Your insecurity will cause you to dig up dirt of their past to validate your resentment of their prosperity. You become very comfortable and dissatisfied. All because you're ignorantly living below your privilege as a King's Kid!

God made all of us to be blessed! When our brothers or sisters in Christ increase, we also increase. It's a shame for any one to get an attitude because somebody happens to get what God said they ought to have gotten all along. We know how some of us do: "Honey, do you see the way she's acting since she got that new car? She thinks she's better than us. Do you see how high she rides with her head up?" It isn't that she's riding with her head up so high, its just that her old car sat low, and the new car sits high. The springs in the old car were shot, and God has given her a decent seat! And no, she's not ignoring you, but she's busy listening to her praise and worship music! She's so appreciative of God's blessing in her life because her old car didn't have a tape player! And yet you have an attitude thinking she's ignoring you and she's going down the road enjoying God!

Here's another familiar complaint: "Have you seen the pastor? How in the world can he afford to drive a Cadillac and all his members take the bus?" The truth is if your pastor drove a Pinto, you wouldn't have a problem. But whether it hurts you or not, your pastor is not called to drive anything that's smoking or degrading! He's serving God, and God blesses His servants! Besides which, the shepherd is always supposed to be more prosperous than the sheep. It is ludicrous to think that a mail person would be more wealthy than the president or C.E.O. of a corporation!!

Some people attempt to drive God's blessed folks to a place of insanity. Their envying tries to make the blessed ones think that they are losing their mind because they are being blessed. They are caused to feel like they are in sin. Yet, we don't have any problem with the unbeliever owning multi-billion dollar corporations, airlines, etc. Can't you see that is foolish? Well friend, whether your attitude can handle it or not, and whether your ego can make the adjustment or not, God said that He blessed His people and commanded that they stay blessed.

One more thing....I don't care what is said; you can't curse what God has blessed! I clearly remember once meeting with some board members of a committee that I'm a part of and an accusation began to appear. "Bishop Mellette, they tell us that you don't have many members in your church living over there in the projects anymore. They say they don't come to your church anymore." I said, "Brother, you need to check the record. There is some truth to that because we don't have a lot of members from that area coming to the church now. We have taught them well and they have moved out. They live in homes now and what they used to sit around and wait to receive as their sustenance for one month, they now make on the job every week. They just don't live there anymore."

Now if teaching people to do better is a crime, I'm guilty. Very, very guilty!!! If teaching people to feel better about themselves is a crime, them I'm guilty. If teaching people that they can have and do more and be better, I'm guilty. If helping people to think higher and greater is a sin, then I'm guilty. And I don't mind being charged "Guilty, guilty, guilty!" As a matter of fact, the Bible says, "Count it all joy when men revile you and persecute you and say all manner of evil against you falsely for My sake. Rejoice and be exceedingly glad." It's a pleasure to have folk to try to curse what God has blessed because it just simply tells me we've got to be doing something right!

CHAPTER II

MULTIPLY AND WAX EXCEEDINGLY MIGHTY

Jesus taught the law of multiplication, which must be grasped, in order for anyone to walk in the full measure of the prosperity appointed unto them. Our minds must be renewed to His methods of prosperity. Our hearts must be in earnest expectation that He rewards those who diligently seek Him. We can't have a mind set of lack, of poverty or "only" to come into prosperity. Everybody thinks about addition and subtraction -- which would you prefer, money to be added or subtracted to your bank account? What would you prefer, your finances to multiply or divide? The answer is obvious...whatever it takes to add more zeros behind the decimal point. God wants to elevate our level of thinking. Elevate the vastness of our mind and understand that God is not limited to addition...but He multiplies! We are looking for 2 when God is giving 20!

I once was sharing with someone what God put in my spirit about what He wanted to do for them. They had already decided that they wanted to get a good job and that they were going to pursue an education for two years and then get a better job. God said to tell them He wasn't going to waste 2 years waiting to bless their life. God said He was going to cause them to obtain what they thought the school would give them. That brings us to another point: when it comes down to blessings, your covenant with God is the only requirement you need. He'll place you in positions that you are unqualified for in the natural, but because of your spiritual qualifications, He can place them into your hands. There is a law of multiplication that God is waiting for you to comprehend and apprehend. Your obedience will produce multiplication in your life.

> **And God blessed them, and God said unto them, Be fruitful, and multiply, and replenish the earth, and subdue it: and have dominion over the fish of the sea, and over the fowl of the air, and over every living thing that moveth upon the earth.**
>
> **Genesis 1:28**

There is a second law; the law of acquisition. God commanded man to subdue the land. He said that they were to go and acquire what He had set up for them. They had to "go." Unfortunately, most people in the church are sitting back with their legs crossed waiting to hit the lottery...making soda companies rich hoping to get the red hot number. Don't put your hope in such worldly systems of acquisition! God has a preordained method for your prosperity. One way is through tithing. Pay your tithes, you'll hit the number! The number is 10; ten percent. The hot number is 10%; every time you hit that target you win!! And when you go over into the offering, the 11th percent, God takes notice and begins to pour out the blessings that you can't have room enough to receive it.

Bring ye all the tithes into the storehouse, that there may be meat in mine house, and prove me now herewith, saith the LORD of hosts, if I will not open you the windows of heaven, and pour you out a blessing, that there shall not be room enough to receive it.

And I will rebuke the devourer for your sakes, and he shall not destroy the fruits of your ground; neither shall your vine cast her fruit before the time in the field, saith the LORD of hosts.

And all nations shall call you blessed: for ye shall be a delightsome land, saith the LORD of hosts.

Malachi 3:10-12

That is a reality! You know you are walking in the Malachi 3 life when you have more cars than you can drive at one time, more homes than you can live in at one time, more money than you can hold in one bank securely at one time and more clothes than you can possibly wear in a lifetime.

There is a third law that you must understand; the law of order and authority. He said to them, "have dominion over the creation," which meant, "as long as God was Lord over them they would have dominion under Him." What does it mean to have dominion? Wherever Jesus Christ is Lord, that is His domain. So we keep Him Lord over what we do. This also meant that they had the responsibility of carrying out structure and order in the earth. In other words, God made earth for man, not man for earth. God did not make man to serve the earth but rather God made the earth to serve the man.

Everything in the earth should obey your command to benefit and not harm you. Dominion means you walk in wealth, because the trees that make money are subject to you. The earth that brings forth diamonds is subject to you and the sea that brings forth pearls is subject to you. You have dominion; you have the ability to cut down the tree, dig up the earth and scan the sea.

If you're driving down the highway and the speed limit is 35 and you're doing 70 miles per hour and you see the highway patrolman sitting down there, what are you going to do? If you're smart, you'll slow down. He doesn't have to get out of his car and put his hand out and say slow down. He doesn't have to turn on his lights. No! The moment you see that car, what do you do? Slow down. Why? Because you recognize the authority that is in force.

God wants to teach you the same law in every area. When you are working and serving and obeying God, you'll walk in His authority. When the devil is coming your way, and you put your hand up, he will cease and desist, for he understands you are clothed in God's authority. He has to stop whatever he is doing, and recognize your authority. He has to cease and desist his demonic activities, or he'll get pulled over. But the only way the devil responds to that is when he knows that you are obeying God and you are in consistent obedience to God. How does the devil know when we are being obedient to God? He knows because you are not working with him; you're on the opposing team. And when you say, "stop," he has to stop because you are not a part of his team. You are wearing a different uniform than his. You have power over him. Your obedience is the patrol car that signals possible imprisonment if he doesn't abide by your authority. That's a powerful truth!

Now, people that are living any kind of way can't make the devil stop. You know why? Because the devil says, "I isn't stopping, 'cause you are a part of me. You are on my team. You are wearing the same uniform as I. Now how are you going to tell me what to do? You forgot, I am your daddy." But when you are living for the Lord and the devil shows up you can say, "Hold it, I'm over you. Get behind me. Get under my feet. I'm the boss." The Bible says, "Submit yourselves therefore unto God...resist the devil and he will flee." (James 4:7) When we are obedient and submissive to God, we can resist the devil and he will flee.

God saw Adam and Eve as vessels of honor. Look again at Genesis, chapter one, verse 31. *"And God saw everything that He had made and behold it was very good and the evening and the morning were the sixth day."* God saw them as vessels of honor. There was no disobedience and man was in love with God. God looked at them and they were good.

In chapter two of Genesis, the Bible says, *"And the Lord God formed man of the dust of the ground and breathed into his nostrils the breath of life and man became a living soul and the Lord God planted a garden eastward in Eden and therefore He put the man whom He had formed."* And verse 9 says, *"And out of the ground made the Lord God to grow every tree that is pleasant to the sight and good for food. The tree of life also in the midst of the garden and the tree of knowledge of good and evil."* We have God's breath in us. We have the blood of God running in our veins. We are a living soul. Now we know how to glorify God and we understand that we have a God to glorify and a soul to be saved.

God can house His anointing and His power inside of man because He's breathing into man and he has been made in His Image.

MULTIPLY AND WAX EXCEEDINGLY MIGHTY

There were two trees that stood in the garden. One was the tree of life, the other the tree of knowledge of good and evil. Now, the tree of life pertained to and contained all things for man to live forever. Access to this tree was based upon a proper relationship with God. The tree of knowledge of good and evil served as a test of man's obedience to God. God did not use it to tempt the man, for the Bible clearly says God tempts no man. The tree was there to test and to see how loyal man would always be to God. God doesn't tempt you to do evil, but He does permit a test to determine how loyal you really are. God doesn't try to get you to do something just to prompt you to do something wrong. No. God permits things to come so you can present to Him how much you love Him by not getting involved.

The same real questions that faced Adam and Eve faces us today. When difficulty arises, so do two questions: (1) which path should be chosen?, and, (2) what kind of relationship do you want with God?. No matter what comes against you, and no matter what confronts you, the first question will always be, "Which path should be chosen?"

And the Lord God took the man and put him into the Garden of Eden to dress it and to keep it and the Lord God commanded the man saying, of every tree of the garden thou mayest freely eat, but of the tree of the knowledge of good and evil, thou shalt not eat of it: for in the day that thou eatest thereof, thou shalt surely die.

Genesis 2:15-17

This Scripture represents a direct command. At the issuance, the devil is not living in man's life because man is obeying God. There is no sign of disobedience, but God gave the command not to eat of the tree and said that the day you eat of it you are going to surely die. Let us follow closely to what is taking place.

Verse 18 says, *"And the Lord God said, it is not good that man should be alone. I will make him a help meet for him." God said "I'm going to make somebody to help him. God said "I'm going to give man someone to improve him, make him better, and make him great." In other words, God looked at him and said, "He needs some help."*

Verse 19 says, *"And out of the ground the Lord God formed every beast of the field and every fowl of the air and brought them unto Adam to see what he would call them. And whatsoever Adam called every living creature, that was the name thereof and Adam gave names to all the cattle and to the fowl of the air and to every beast of the field but for Adam there was not found a help meet for him."* Among the creatures, there was no one to improve him.

But, God had a solution. Verse 21: *"And the Lord God caused a deep sleep to fall upon Adam and he slept and he took one of his ribs and closed up the flesh instead thereof and the rib which the Lord God had taken from man made He a woman and brought her unto the man."*

No matter what the state of the man is, when God deals with him, He puts the man to sleep. When He is through with him, he is different. God took part of Adam's rib cage, which is used to protect his vital organs. Adam doesn't even know what's going on. He's out cold having a good time sleeping.

Eve was made for protection. The woman was anointed to protect the man; to improve him. Then, God goes back and awakens Adam. "Wake up son! Get up! Check this out!"

Adam is left with a choice. "Do I or do I not want what God has brought me?" God brought her, but He didn't make Adam take her. The man had to decide to take her. Some of us say, "God made me take that woman. God made me take that man." No! You made the decision.

Verse 22. *"And the rib which the Lord God had taken from man, made He a woman and brought her unto him." The woman was presented to man as a gift from God, and like man, she was good and perfect. But, Adam still had to decide what he was going to do. Adam looks at her and then he made his choice. He said, "Woman, you are bone of my bone and flesh of my flesh. You are going to be called Woman because you were taken out of me." In essence, he was saying, "I choose you." "Therefore shall a man leave his father and his mother and shall cleave unto his wife and they shall be one flesh."*

31

He said, "My God, I have got to have her. Can you see it? Bone of my bone. Flesh of my flesh. My woman!" He looked at God. "I leave my mama and my daddy. I forget about biscuits, gravy and everything for you to give me something like this!" Yes, Adam chose her.

And Eve, if you can imagine, said, "Man, you just made the best choice you ever made in your life, 'cause I'm going to touch you where no cow, no monkey, no hippo or animal has been able to touch you before! I'm going to make your liver quiver, your intestines and everything else jump because I came out of the inside of you. I know more about the inside of you than you know about yourself. I know just where to touch and tickle you." The woman came out of the man. That's how come she knows how to make him feel good. She knew more about his insides than he did!

Everything was in harmony; in order and sweet. And the Bible says they were both naked. The man and his wife and were not ashamed because there was no sin or disobedience that would spark the element of shame. They were pure and clean in the eyesight of God and everything was wonderful and great. They could walk together because they were in agreement. They could enjoy the benefits of the garden, because they were in divine order. They were obedient and at this point the devil had no place in them.

CHAPTER III

OBEDIENCE IS COSTLY

There is a price to be paid for success and maintaining it often requires education.

Why do we, as believers, often bite on and devour our successful brothers and sisters? We must not give in to the demonically instilled, collective mentality of divisiveness. We must take a stand in unity for God -- that is His original plan.

God made every one of us unique in our own way. However, the devil has planted a vain imagination in the hearts of men that causes us to feel threatened by that very uniqueness. If we are not aware of God's plan, We will devour one another.

There are three truths you should always remember:

1. The devil does not want you to have a relationship with God.

2. The devil is cursed by God.

3. The devil can't stop God from forgiving you.

People have gotten into trouble because they went somewhere they shouldn't, or they did something that they knew was wrong. How many times have you known people who have died because they stepped somewhere they shouldn't have? Your location with respect to the boundaries that God sets for you is very important. God never sets boundaries for you to ignore or overlook them. Getting out of line may cost you your life! If Satan can just get you to step outside of your God-given boundaries, he has already set you up for a fall.

The dictionary defines death as "the loss of life," "the state of being dead," and "a state in which one has no more control." Make the devil dead in our life; declare him to be in a state where he has no control over you. If you think the devil has control over you after God has delivered you, you will always be subject to his prophecies of defeat. You would be surprised at the number of people in the church whom God has already delivered, and they are still listening to the devil tell them he still has them. They haven't received the truth --

34

that they have overcome. Sadly, they believe the father of lies more than they believe the Spirit of Truth!

The enemy may say, "Well, that's OK. You didn't do it yesterday, but you're going to do it tomorrow. You haven't gotten over it." God's Word says, "You are more than a conqueror!" Renew your mind or forever live in bondage. When God has delivered you, you don't have to do it tomorrow. God brought you out of it today, therefore, you are over it. It's a done deal. It's over. That stronghold has been toppled; it is void of power.

Ye are of your father, the devil and the lust of your father ye will do.
John 8:44

That defeated foe, the devil, was a murderer from the beginning and abode not in the truth because there is no truth in him. When he speaks a lie, he speaks of his own. The devil lies to promote himself and his program. He lies to entice you and to get your participation in the things he plans to use to destroy mankind. He speaks and tells lies of his own. Get it in your mind: he is a liar and the father of all lies.

Anyone who lives for the devil will lie and distort the truth. Liars are living in the image of their father. Judas had to kiss Jesus so the men who came to arrest Him would know who He was -- His disciples walked, talked and looked so much like Jesus, they couldn't tell them apart. When we

35

spend time in His presence, we begin to live, walk, talk and act like Him.

When the enemy encountered Eve in the garden, the first thing he did was to tell a lie -- to warp the truth -- "Yea, hath God said ..." We know he can talk because he's spoken to every one of us at one time or another. He will always try to get us to question what we know God has said, to act independently and against God's will for our lives. Jesus answered him with His Word and that is what we should do. Resist him and dismiss him with God's Word.

Satan's strategy is to launch an attack against your mind. He tried to plant doubt into the spirit of Eve, this woman of God so that she would disbelieve what God had told her. Does this sound familiar? Perhaps when you came to church and were born again, before you could leave, the enemy showed up and told you, "You're not saved." Maybe when you gave your life to God, before you could get out of the church parking lot, the devil told you, "You're not going to change." What is he doing? He is trying to propagate doubt in your mind, to get you to listen to him. Do not doubt. Hold on to the truth, even if you have to rehearse it, write it down or record it. Keep the truth before your eyes and in your ears to help keep you on the road to obedience.

Not only will Satan try to make you doubt, he will try to distract you by engaging you in conversation. Satan's question opened the door for Eve to talk back to the serpent.

You've got to talk back to the devil, but it must be in such a way that it produces victory in your life. Never deal with an enemy on his own turf. Wait until you are on your own battlefield, then wage war successfully. By fighting him on his turf, you set yourself up for a fall. Eve agreed with the serpent and said, "Yes, we may eat of the fruit of the tree of the garden, but of the fruit of the tree which is in the midst of the garden, God hath said ye shall not eat of it, neither shall you touch it, lest you die." Not only did she agree with the fact that she was not supposed to eat it, but she went ahead to open another door and give the devil some more headway. She told him some more of God's business. She said not only are we not supposed to eat it, but if we touch it, we will die.

Too many people today are being defeated because the devil knows too much about their business. Loose lips sink ships. Eve's lips testified against her. Every time you open your mouth, you may be setting yourself up for destruction. There are some things that happen in your life of which you must repent. You get them right and get them straight with God and that's between you and God. So many people's lives have been destroyed because they got up in church to testify and divulged personal information. Rather than using that information to help, someone took it outside the church. Don't tell the church your business. Not all church goers love God. When I first started going to church, I didn't love God. I had some other things on my mind. I thought I'd go there and check out what was going on, and see if there was anything in there that I could get.

When you go to church with the spirit of the devil, you just come to steal, kill or destroy. Some people, when they first come to church, don't come because they just love God, nor do they come because they feel this dramatic urge that they have to be in there. No way! They come in as a thief to steal, kill or destroy.

The devil took full advantage of the information Eve gave him. And the serpent said unto the woman, "Ye shall not truly die." That was an outright, bold-face lie that contradicted what God had already made clear to her. His plan was to get her to break her focus, and it worked. God's focus was for them not to touch the tree of good and evil, and the devil came to tell her to touch it and break her focus. The devil wants to break your focus...to get you off track...to get you sidelined...to get you to deviate away from the things that God has called and appointed you to do. If the devil can break your focus, he'll destroy your life. People fall and hurt themselves because of broken focus. All men fall...but great men and women get back up. Which one are you?

One moment, Eve was in obedience to God and the devil had no place in her life. He could do nothing with her. The very next moment, however, she was in a state of disobedience to God. That's how quickly it can happen. A few moments of broken focus and she fell from her state of glory with God. By getting her to disobey God, Satan got a foothold in her spirit. The devil wants to do the same thing to us. He searches for a foothold in our spirit to temporarily separate us from God and His provision. "For God doth know that in the day you eat thereof, then your eyes shall be opened and ye shall be as gods, knowing good and evil."

The devil is real (Isaiah 14). Nonetheless, you don't have to agree or argue with him. If God has told us it's true, we don't need the devil to talk to us about it. If God tells you to do something, why in the world would you go to the devil to find out whether or not you should do it? If God told you to do something, then why do you need somebody else's approval to do it? If you come to me and say, "Pastor Mellette, God spoke to me last night in a dream. He told me to fast for three days, and I want to know what you have to say about it?" Now, what do you think I should say? If God told you to fast, why do you want to know what I have to say about it? That's between you and God! Don't get me mixed up with that! What do you want me to do, tell you He didn't say it? What do you want me to do, tell you He did say it? I wasn't there when you had the dream! You told me that He told you! You've got a bunch of people walking around in the church talking about what God told them to do and every time you turn around, they're asking somebody about what God told them. They forget that their allegiance and obedience is and should only be to God. Vain is the help of man.

Confusion abounds when you try to confirm God's counsel. That's why people are confused, mixed up and walking around blindly. They have unwittingly opened themselves up to false prophecies simply because they went and asked someone else to confirm God's instructions. What in the world is an unsaved person going to do with a saved person's problem? If you're having problems with your husband and God speaks to you and tells you to love him more, why are you going to go to the psychiatrist and see whether or not you need to love him more? God told you to love him more -- that should be the end of the matter. God is the Alpha and Omega. If you believe Him, He'll give you the beginning and the end of any matter.

God told you what to do, and you're still dialing the 900 number trying to get a hold of a psychic to see whether or not God really said it. If you just believe God...you can keep your money in your pocket...and you won't have that great big ole phone bill. What if your phone bill could testify? What would it say about your allegiance to God?

How art thou fallen from heaven, oh Lucifer, son of the morning. How are thou cut down to the ground, which didst weaken the nation.

For thou hath said in thine heart, I will ascend into heaven, I will exalt my throne above the stars of God, I will sit also upon the mount of the congregation, in the sides of the north:

I will ascend above the heights of the clouds; I will be like the most High.

Yet, thou shall be brought down to hell, to the sides of the pit."

Isaiah 14:12-15

When comparing these verses to Genesis 3, it is possible to see why the devil wanted Eve to eat of that fruit. He realized that she would be as God, knowing good and evil. Satan wanted her to be like him, to possess an exalted, lifted up and prideful spirit. He wanted to be God himself. He knew that if he could get man to disobey God, man would begin to think of himself as a god and wouldn't need God. That is what has happened and that is what man has done. Since that day, man has been building and trying to build systems, organizations and institutions that don't need God to operate. Man has tried to become his own god and he has failed miserably.

That is why the devil wants us to disobey God, because then we start taking control of our own lives and you're telling God, "I don't need Your direction to make it. I know what's best for me." Look at what happened to the devil -- he got kicked out of heaven. Disobedience will cause you to be thrown out of the sphere of blessings into a dismal pit of cursings.

In Genesis 3:5, the devil told Adam and Eve a lie that caused their separation from the true and the living God. He wanted man to do what he had done. Verse 6 says, "And when the woman saw that the tree was good for food and that it was pleasant to the eyes and a tree to be desired to make one wise, she took up the fruit thereof and did eat and gave also unto her husband with her and he did eat." Apparently Eve's focus was broken -- she had to have been close to the tree. The Bible said she looked at it and saw it was good. When she did, the devil talked her into doing something she shouldn't have done. One look can change your life forever. One look turned Lot's wife into a pillar of salt. One look made King David kill a man to get his wife. Watch your eyes! [*"After she ate thereof, and did eat, she gave also unto her husband with her."*] Adam was right there while this was going on. Some contend that the fall would not have happened if Adam had been there, if he had been in his place. The Bible says he was with her. She gave it to him and he did eat. The man was just as guilty as the woman, for more reasons than one. He was the head of Eve. In the natural body the mouth is in the head. As the head, he could have prevented the mouth from eating. He did not. As the head, he could have prevented the mouth from engaging in conversation with the serpent, but he did not. Thus, because the head was not functioning according to divine purpose, the entire body suffered!

A look at Romans One reveals some things. There are a bunch of men running around putting their problems on the woman. "If you women..." "If Eve hadn't ever..." If Eve hadn't this and Eve hadn't that, Adam wouldn't have this and Adam wouldn't have that, then why didn't Adam call her into question? After all, she did not pull out a .9 millimeter and make him eat it. Men must stop blaming women for their problems. As the head, they must take responsibility and yield control in every situation. The brain, the control mechanism, is in the head. Men take control of your lives, your situations, and your homes.

For this cause God gave them up unto vile affections: for even their women did change the natural use into that which is against nature:

And likewise also the men, leaving the natural use of the woman, burned in their lust one toward another; men with men working that which is unseemly, and receiving in themselves that recompence of their error which was meet.

Romans 1:26-27

This Scripture speaks of homosexuality and lesbianism. Men left the natural use of the women and turned to the men. Women left the natural use of the men and turned to other women. God's plan was for woman and man. Anything else is an abomination of the will and purpose of God. Everything was clean and pure. Now they've disobeyed and God says, "Look out." There are men who have been deceived by the devil into thinking they are supposed to go to bed with other men. Beware of these men. Some of these men will marry a woman and then go to bed with their uncle. That's tight, but it's right! Husbands and wives are supposed to enjoy each other. How do you think you got here?

And likewise also the men, leaving the natural use of the woman, burned in their lust one toward another; men with men working that which is unseemly and receiving in themselves that recompense of their error which was met.

And even as they did not like to retain God in their knowledge, God gave them over to a reprobate mind, to do those things which are not convenient;

Being filled with all unrighteousness, fornication, wickedness, covetousness, maliciousness, full of envy, murder, debate, deceit, malignity; whispers,

Backbiters, haters of God, despiteful, proud, boasters, inventors of evil things, disobedient to parents,

Without understanding, covenant breakers, without natural affection, implacable, and unmerciful

Romans 1:27-31

When you try to be your own god, you fall into all kinds of sin. You become detrimental to yourself, to others and to society. Instead of being a sweet savor in the nostrils of God, you become a strange fire that evokes His wrath.

And for those of you who thought Adam was innocent, look at verse 32:

Who knowing the judgment of God [God told him first with her] that they which commit such things are worthy of death [Eve was worthy of death, not because she ate] not only that those that do the same, but those that have pleasure in them that do it."

You don't have to do it, but when you take pleasure in those that do do it, you're worthy of the same death. "Oh, honey, he's a homosexual and it's in his genes." "Just leave him alone; it's just a disease." Stop saying that it's only a disease. That's a lie. Homosexuality is a conscious choice to sin against God's original intent for mankind. It's devilish. And, further, it is more than "just a little white lie." The Word of God says it is an abomination.

Even if you don't do it, check yourself. Do you take pleasure in people who do things they ought not? I would not be a decent, respectful pastor, friend and man of God to you if I saw you doing wrong, walking in error and about to make a mistake, and I did not stop you. I am commissioned to say, "Hold it. You're going the wrong way." People who see you willfully walk in disobedience and do not correct you are not doing you a favor. They are only hurting you. People walk past and won't talk about the filthiness and the ugliness of unrighteousness, but if you are ever going to be what God wants you to be, you're going to have to hear somebody tell you the cold, hard truth. Someone has got to inflict the pain of change. You don't need the root worker...you don't need the sorcerer...you don't need no roots, no rabbit's foot...no lucky charm, or the four-leaf clover...all you need to do is obey God. Obedience is all you need to stay on the right track, always walking in the light of the revealed Word of God.

Satan delights in our disobedience because he doesn't want us to have a relationship with God. The Bible says that after they sinned, Adam and Eve made aprons. It was a poor excuse for a covering, for man cannot heal himself of sin. The aprons signified Adam and Eve's attempt to cover up their sin. However, sin can not be covered up. Sin must be forgiven!

And they heard the voice of the Lord God walking in the garden in the cool of the day and Adam and his wife hid themselves from the presence of the Lord God amongst the trees of the garden. And the Lord God called unto Adam and said unto him, Where art thou? And he said, I heard thy voice in the garden, and I was afraid, because I was naked; and I hid myself. And he said, Who told thee that thou wast naked. Hast thou eaten of the tree whereof I commanded thee that though shouldest not eat? And the man said, The woman whom thou gavest to be with me, she gave me of the tree and I did eat. And the Lord God said unto the woman, What is this that thou hast done? And the woman said, the serpent beguiled me, and I did eat. Now the woman is passing the buck. It wasn't me, it was the devil. She said the devil made me do it.

The devil does not want you to have a relationship with God. It's that simple. When disobedience entered in, man's fellowship was broken with God. God came walking in the cool of the day, Adam and Eve ran and hid themselves. What does that say? When you begin to disobey, your relationship with God begins to be broken. It is almost like being on the telephone talking to somebody, and in the midst of talking all of a sudden something goes "click." Disobedience will cause your line of communication to be cut off. Adam and Eve knew they were wrong and when God showed up, they didn't even want to be around God.

The devil, of course, was ecstatic. He felt he had achieved his ultimate goal -- but he was wrong. Thank God! God said, "Where are you?" Wherever God puts us, He expects to find us there in the end. So when God first saved you, He expects you still to be saved. God doesn't want to come and say, "Where are you?" When God calls you to do something, or when God calls you to be a part of something don't let God have to ask where you are.

Obedience is not only a heart condition, it is a position, a placing. Be in your rightful place. There are too many people who have moved out of their rightful place. Adam and Eve had figuratively and literally moved out of the place of obedience. They were disjointed. God did not linger on their placement. He wanted to know the source of their disobedience. "Did somebody tell you, or did you eat?" So God said, "Who told you that thou was naked? Hast thou eaten of the tree which I commanded you not to eat of?" What's done in the dark will come to the light. The Bible says, "All things hidden shall be revealed." You can't cover your sins. The Bible says whoever covers his sins shall not prosper. Some people are hung up, stuck on the same level, because they are trying to cover up something...they need to give it to God.

You can't keep making excuses. Everyone's passing the buck. You got too many people in the church walking around saying "The devil made me do it." The devil is not omnipotent -- he cannot be everywhere at the same time. And he doesn't have enough staff persons -- demons -- to be everywhere. "Oh, child, I had a flat tire; that devil, he tried to stop me. But I just told him he wasn't going to stop me." "Child, I was coming to the church, got right near the church, and ran out of gas. Lord, the devil tried to get in my gas tank." That wasn't the devil; that was you. You were negligent.

All too often, we give the devil credit for events in which he was never involved. And by doing so, we inadvertently give him a form of praise that only belongs unto God. We must acknowledge our own shortcomings and stop blaming every little thing on the devil. God has given us a unique ability to think and make decisions, for which we must be held accountable. Yet it is through the grace of God that we are overcomers. We are bound to render praise unto God, and in all things to give Him thanks.

Revelations 4:11 "Thou art worthy, O Lord, to receive glory and honor and power; for thou hast created all things; and for thy pleasure they are and were created".

The devil does not want us to have a relationship with God because he knows that you and I are a source of pleasure to God. In other words, we turn God on. We make God feel good. We can give God something that the devil can't give him. We can be to God what the devil can never be to Him again.

Satan is cursed by God for evermore (Genesis 3:14). Adam said Eve made me do it; Eve said the devil made me do it. Now God is going down to the devil. He is getting down to the source of the problem.

"And the Lord God said unto the serpent, Because thou hast done this, thou art cursed above all the cattle, and above every beast of the field; upon thy belly shalt thou go, and dust shalt thou eat all the days of thy life. And the Lord God formed man of the dust of the ground, and breathed into his nostrils the breath of life; and man became a living soul.

What did God make man out of? The dust. When God cursed the devil, what did God say he'd eat the rest of his life? The dust. The devil will constantly eat of the flesh of men and women for the rest of his life. And the only way the devil will not eat of you is when you get out of the flesh and into the spirit. Isn't it interesting that he will eat the rest of his life of the very thing you and I are made out of? He has an open door to people who are in the flesh, but a closed door to people who are in the spirit. Galatians 5:16: "This I say then, Walk in the Spirit and ye shall not fulfill the lust of the flesh." In other words, get out of the flesh, get into the Spirit, and the devil won't be able to do anything with you. Verse 17: "For the flesh lusteth against the Spirit and the Spirit against the flesh and these are contrary the one to the other: so that ye cannot do the things that ye would."

The Spirit wants to please God and the only way to keep the devil from eating away at your life is to get out of the flesh and get into the Spirit. That's why obedience is so important. *"But the fruit of the Spirit is love, joy, peace, longsuffering, gentleness, goodness and faith, meekness, temperance: against such there is no law."* You live by these things when you get out of the flesh, when you get into the realm of the Spirit, fruit will be produced in your life.

The devil can't do anything with people who live in the realm of the God's Spirit, and who possess these attributes. These characteristics keep the devil away from you.

Look at Psalms 103:14. "For he knoweth our frame, he remembereth that we are dust." That's saying the Lord knows our frame and He remembers that we are but dust. Yet God loves us. Through all of our faults and mixed motives, God continues to love us. The devil can never stop God from forgiving you. He can't stand against the love of God. Genesis 3:21 After all is said and done, the Bible says, "And God said unto Adam and also unto his wife that the Lord God did make coats of skins and did clothe them." In the midst of everything that was done and in the midst of everything that took place, God forgave them. The clothes that God put on them were significant of the fact that He forgave them and gave them a fresh start. No matter what you've been up against, and no matter what the devil tries to get you to do, God is a forgiver and He will give you a fresh start.

CHAPTER IV

OBEDIENCE: THE CALL & PURPOSE OF LIFE

God has one purpose for your obedience: to develop you into a receptacle for his love, mercy, grace and blessing. Simply put, the end result of obedience is to get you to the place in your life where you acknowledge the importance of His instruction and the importance of your compliance with His instructions. When you obey God, you eliminate a whole lot of distractions, sorrows, wrong turns and shattered dreams that otherwise might have crept into your life. Also, you eliminate down time, the time necessary to bounce back from broken focus that occurs when you disobey God.

When we get to the place where we willingly embrace obedience to God, we will understand it and celebrate its proper place in our lives. We will prosper. Recall the state you were in before you were born again. Back then, you didn't understand all the hype about giving your life to Jesus. Actually, you deemed it a waste of time. How do I know? Because if you would have understood the benefits, the joys and the blessing of salvation, you would have received Christ the very first time He was introduced to you. Now that you are born again, you understand why so many people kept harping, "You need to be born again." "Jesus is the Reason for the season." "Jesus is the Center of my joy." Now you understand, because you are experiencing the rewards of obedience to the call of salvation. Most likely, if you're like many, there have been many times that you have asked yourself "why did I wait so long?"

When you embrace the call to obedience, a light goes on that says, "This is the smartest thing I have ever done." Even in the midst of trials, you understand that because of your obedience, you are walking with the One who said, "Many are the afflictions of the righteous, but I deliver them from them all." With that surety, you can walk through the valley of the shadow of death fearing no evil because He is walking you through with His rod and staff protecting you.

In Isaiah 1, the Bible reveals that in the very beginning of time, the devil talked mankind into going against God. He created a communication problem between God and man. The only way that man could be restored back into communication with God was that man had to be forgiven. The path of forgiveness is strewn with the rocks of obedience.

Sometimes you will make mistakes. Sometimes you will do things wrong. Sometimes you will open your mouth to say things that you wish you hadn't. Have you ever wished sometimes your mouth had stayed closed? I've been there. Hardly a day goes by that I don't wish I had kept my mouth closed. It's easier to say nothing and bite the bullet of frustration and anger than it is to repent to man and God after hurting someone's feelings or saying something unwholesome. The Bible clearly teaches that nothing should proceed out of our mouths except that which edifies the hearer. Even with our words, therefore, obedience is better than sacrifice.

Forgiveness is the road of restoration back to God. When disobedience developed, Adam and Eve could not walk the way they used to. They understood they had to be covered. However, the fig leaves that they used ended up being too small. The leaves were unable to cover their hearts, or penetrate their minds. They were unable to prevent Adam and Eve from being brought to their knees before God. Besides which, like a king to a subject, God had to invite them into His Presence. He had to hold out the golden scepter of favor that indicated, "You may come to Me." God had to forgive man. That simply means, when you do something that you shouldn't, you should just ask God to forgive you.

A lie that rests among the devil's arsenal is that forgiveness is real hard and real difficult. He wants you to think it will take so many "Hail Mary's," so many days and hours of fasting and prayer, and so much work before God forgives you. That, my friend, is a lie from the very depths of the pit of hell! The Bible is clear from Genesis to Revelation that forgiveness is easily accessible by repenting of the sin and asking God to forgive you. Take words with you, go before God and in your own manner just say, "God, I goofed. I acknowledge I did . . . I am sorry. Please forgive me." That's it. Then as you repent -- turn in the opposite direction of that sin -- and come back into the place of obedience. You are restored into fellowship with God.

Take, as an example, a brother who has sinned. God has told him to come all the way over to this door. The first thing that the devil will do is begin to distract and attack him to try to keep him from getting to that door. When he can't stop him from reaching the door, he'll try another tactic. The devil plots, "If I can't attack you and slow you down to keep you from getting to the door, then I'm gonna try to push you too fast so you will skip stages that are crucial to your development in the process of trying to get to the door." If that doesn't work, he has a third trick up his sleeve. When the Christian is going through different things and up against different opposition, the devil will beat him over the head all the time, telling him, "You haven't got to that door yet. You aren't doing what God told you to do. You aren't ever gonna get there." He will keep bringing to this brother's mind all the times he slipped, all the times he failed, and all the times he supposedly let God down.

Let me just say here, there is no way you can ever let God down. Remember, God is the one who said "vain is the help of man." If God told man that, do you think he is relying on man for anything? Of course not. So stop putting yourself down -- and up! You need God more than he needs you and God is in control of you and not vice versa. Relax in that fact and walk upright before Him. In the example with the door, God is not looking at how quick the brother can get to that door. God is not even looking at the fact that he hasn't gotten to the door yet. What God is looking at is that he is making steps toward the door. All God sees is the footprints of obedience on the pathway to the door. Sometimes, something will happen that will hinder the brother or slow him down. God does not get upset; He knows what things will happen. The Omnipotent God has already seen the obstacles ahead and is prepared to turn the stumbling blocks into stepping stones. All God wants the brother to do is to keep making steps toward the door.

Sometimes, the brother may fall or may bruise himself. Again, God looks at that, sees it all. God knows that he will fall but God says, "OK, my son, get up. Don't worry about the fall. Let's keep walking toward the door."

The key to your life is not to focus on the mistakes that you make, nor to focus on how long it takes you to get to a certain place, but rather to focus on the fact that you are making steps to get to where you ought to be. Some of us are not everything that we ought to be. You're not exactly where you should be, but look at how far you have already come. Some of us are too hard on ourselves; we're beating ourselves to death rather than giving ourselves credit for the good that we have done. God sees it and so does the devil. And the devil will have you look at all that you have not done, rather than look at what you have done.

LEARN TO DO WELL

When we do what God wants us to do, the devil has no place in our life. Conversely, when we do what God does not want us to do, then the devil has open season in our life. Isaiah 1:17-19 says that we must, "Learn to do well; seek judgement, relieve the oppressed, judge the fatherless, plead for the widow. Come now, and let us reason together, saith the Lord: though your sins be as scarlet, they shall be as white as snow; though they be red like crimson, they shall be as wool. If ye be willing and obedient, ye shall eat the good of the land."

Obedience affects your everyday life. The Bible says we must learn to do well. Obedience is a process. It does not happen overnight. It takes some time. Don't worry about the mistakes that you make, but rather focus on learning how to get over those mistakes. A mistake is a blessing when you learn from your error and don't allow it to repeat itself. God knew in advance that you would not be able to do everything all at once, so He said, "Listen. You've got to learn to do it." When you get saved, you have to learn how to live saved. When you dedicate your life to the Lord, you must learn how to stay dedicated. People don't get saved today without experiencing problems. They struggle with dilemmas and temptations in their lives and, for some, staying in church is a major battle.

Let me tell you something: living for God everyday is not a simple thing to do. As a matter of fact, sometimes it gets very difficult. Sometimes, it is very difficult to obey everything God wants you to do. Read that.... difficult, but not impossible. For with God all things are possible. So rather than concentrating on getting through every day at one time, let's think about how to get through each day by breaking it down and beginning to think about how to get through each hour. And don't worry about tomorrow, as Matthew 6:25-31 says, for that day will have its own unique set of challenges.

The key to learning to do well is get to the place where you listen to the person who teaches you to do well. We must take the time out every day to hear what God has to say about that day concerning us. When is the best time to pray? When is the best time to hear what God is saying? I think the best time to hear what God is saying is at the beginning of every day, but that's my opinion. The demands of your day may not allow you to begin prayer at 6 a.m., especially if you're working at that time. How would you like to be on a train or bus and your conductor or driver gets on his knees and starts praying while the train is careening out of control? Use wisdom. God has called us to a life of liberty, not bondage.

The main reason I advocate early morning prayer is because it is not very wise to wait to the end of the day to pray about that day, because the day has already passed. So the best thing for you to do and the best thing for me to do is to hear what God has to say about that day before that day begins. That first minute that you wake up should be used to concentrate on giving that first portion of time to God. What do you think would happen to your life if for the next 30 days if you got up, and the first 15 minutes out of every day, before you did anything, you fell on your knees and talked to God? How would you like to hear what God has to say about you every day, every hour of the day? How would you like to be at the right place at the right time, every single hour of your life? How many of us have missed God because we were at the wrong place at the wrong time? How would you like to be everywhere God wants you to be every hour of your life for the next 12 months? You can if you devote time to hear Him. Remember prayer is two-way communication. You're going to have to be quiet and listen. Don't come with a grocery list of items for God to do. Listen to what He wants to fill your empty bag with.

I believe there are many people who have suffered many things in the Church and outside of the Church, simply because they were not where God wanted them to be at a particular time. As a result, they were somewhere they shouldn't have been and something happened that God really did not ordain. It's essential that we eliminate the distractions, the pressures, and the problems in the lives of

God's people by simply getting to where God wants us to be and doing what God wants us to do. The importance of obedience just can't be overstated.

The only way the devil will get in is if we permit him. If we start every day off, without giving God any time, not hearing what He is saying and not learning, guess what? The devil will launch his plan of attack. Now whose plan are we going to allow to operate? Are we going to allow the devil's plan to operate in our life, or are we going to get up every morning and hear what God is saying and undo the devil's plan? Do you not know, if you will give God the first portion of your time every morning, He will reveal to you the hidden traps that the Devil has set for your life that day? He will show you the people that have it in for you that day. He will show you the places that you ought not to go that day. He will tell you who to watch that day. But you've got to give Him time to tell you what it is and who they are. God will tell you every day, every single person that is assigned to bless you that day, if you will listen to Him. God will even get to the place to where He will tell you where to eat lunch and dinner.

Some of the best kept secrets I ever discovered about pleasing and satisfying my wife are the things that God told me to do. One of the best secrets I have found about winning my children to Jesus is what I heard God tell me while I took time to listen to Him. Most of the time, we will go through life with our problems of family, and friends, and loved ones, hoping they will get better and hoping they will go away, when most of the time they don't get better and they don't go away. It's not because God doesn't want them to, but because we will not come before God and hear Him tell us how to get it better. If the devil brings me problems, God must be free to give me solutions. When I don't give God that needed time, I tie Him up and prevent Him from giving me the solution to my problem. God wants me to have the solution, but I've got to give Him the time. We've got to learn. We have to apply ourselves. God is giving you people and putting people around your life to bring out the best in you.

Sometimes the people that God gives you to make you better will inflict the greatest amount of pain in your life. It's like medicine: it's not good going down, but it's the best and quickest cure for the ailment. These individuals poke you where you don't want to be poked; they touch you where you don't want to be touched, and they tell you what you don't want to hear. That is because those are the people designed to make you great and to make you better. Sometimes the people that God gives you to make you better will literally get on your nerves. Do you know why? Because you get tired of them staying on you. Every time you turn around, they are on you about what you need to do, and what you can't do. They are trying to make you better. Sometimes husbands, your wives get on your nerves. You ought to tell the truth. Every man that gets married at some point will find that his wife gets on his nerves. Do you know why that happens? God gave you someone who is designed to bring the best out of you. If she didn't get on your nerves, you would never be what you're supposed to be.

Sometimes you get angry, with wrinkles in your forehead and steam coming out your ears. "I don't like this pressure that the pastor is putting on me; I can't take it, I'm gonna quit." However, quitting won't solve anything. You'll be a half-boiled egg, not good for consumption and the only thing that will be able to stomach you is the garbage.

Pastors push because they know that their sheep have untapped potential. Their job is to make you great. They are forcing you to see that you have more to offer. They are forcing you to see that God wants to do something significant with you. I'm forcing you to w - o - r - k!!! God abhors laziness. We are too lazy to give Him the first portion of our time. We are walking around with His threads on, driving His clean automobiles, living in His fancy apartments and His fancy houses, sitting on His fancy chairs, breathing His air, living on His money, and we don't have time to hear what He has to say after He's done all of that for us.

I don't care if you're not saved. I don't care if you're mowing the lawn or whatever you're doing, you owe God some time. It won't kill you to pray. If you're ashamed of your friends seeing you pray, then you are too ashamed to be blessed. If you must, pray at home when they aren't around. Whatever you do, talk to God. Those of you who are ashamed of prayer, worried about your friends, worried about what they are going to think about you, let me tell you that most of the friends that you are worried about are praying themselves. Some of us prayed more before we were saved than we do now. You need the Lord. You can have all the money in the world, everything may be going fine with no problems, but you know you need God.

The Bible teaches, "learn to do well," and apparently, we have been taught to do wrong. Yes, obedience is a process. All men and women fail at some point. It is the great ones that get back up. Some of the best people in God's service are people who have fallen down, people that have been wounded and abused, walked over or mistreated. Search the Scriptures and you will find that the misfits were God's hand-picked men and women of valor. Even people who have let God down and have failed Him are some of the greatest people that God has created. Learn to do well.

The Bible says, "If you are willing and obedient, you shall eat the good of the land." What does it mean to be willing? I can't force you. I can't make you. God won't force you either -- although He has the might to do so. Like a parent, He wants you to want it. There's nothing like giving your child a present and they jump up and down and tell everyone they can that "Daddy bought me such and such, or "Daddy gave me such and such." It warms your heart so much that you just want to go out and bless that child one more time.

You have to want the blessing; you have to insist that you want it. You must be willing and obedient. If you do what God tells you to do, everything due to you is coming. That's why Habakkuk says to write down the vision because it won't lie, but it will come to pass. The blessing is coming. Jacob saw the angels descending up and down the ladder from heaven. He saw the gifts being passed from the spiritual to the natural realm. He saw in that vision that God was going to manifest some stuff for him that only God, not man, could give him. No wonder he worshiped!

Notice that he did not see any demons on those steps fighting the angels for those packages. No way! There is not a devil in Hell that can keep you from getting what is due you when you do what God tells you to do. There is a mighty move of God. There is something so powerful about the Holy Ghost that God is getting the minds and hearts of our young men and women like never before. The Church had better be ready for this new generation of young people who are coming in because they are coming in knowing the devil is behind them from day one. You're not going to have to prime, pump and beat them to do right. They are coming in militant. They are ready to take territory for the Kingdom. God is doing some awesome things. If you are willing and obedient, you shall eat the good of the land! You shall...not might...but shall!

Learning requires putting forth an effort to study. If you don't read the Bible, how will you know what God is talking about? Understand this: no matter what book you pick up, there is one book that, the moment you pick it up, demons start screaming and do everything to try to force you to put it down and that's the Bible. That's the only book that he doesn't want you to read. He doesn't act up when you're watching TV. He doesn't act up when you're reading "Soap Opera Magazine," the "Enquirer" or any of that stuff. Things don't start running over on the stove when you're reading what inquiring minds want to know. But pick up your Sunday School book, or your Bible. Automatically, he starts to attack you to keep you from reading that book.

I Peter 3:7 talks about the relationship between husbands and wives. He admonishes husbands to dwell with their wives according to knowledge. What this simply means is that you are supposed to know what turns your mate on and what turns your mate off, what makes them happy and what makes them unhappy. But there's another nugget you need to see. You are not only married to your spouse, you are also married to God. Thus, you are to dwell with God according to knowledge. You and I have the responsibility to find out what turns God on and what turns Him off. I cannot dwell with God without knowing what pleases Him and what displeases Him. I have to dwell with Him according to knowledge. The Bible says God's people perish for lack of knowledge.

Ask yourself, "When was the last time I read a good, spiritual book other than the Bible?" Think about it. Do you have money problems? When was the last time you bought a book on how to improve your money management? You got sickness in your body...when was the last time you bought a book on how to be healed? In addition to the Bible, there are other books that you can learn from reading. Invest in yourself. Go to the bookstore and buy something for your mind.

Young sisters who are entertaining marriage like to see young men who have nice cars, but they also want you to have something between your ears. Before I got saved, I thought as long as a car was clean, the music was loud, the windows were tinted and I could half dress, I had it. But when I met my wife, I found out she was looking for more than that from a man. She wanted a man with some brains. Being cool won't pay the bills. Having the right kind of haircut won't pay the bills. Looking sweet and nice won't pay the bills. Riding around in your shiny car, even if it is the cleanest one in town, won't pay the bills.

Times are changing. Women are requiring more. They have a right to. Why settle for second best...when you can insist on the best? And I am praying to God that you women put a little more pressure on us men to make us better. If you really want to know the truth about it, we've got it a little bit too easy. Most men are big babies anyway. "Honey, my back...right here...my back, baby." What about when her back hurts? Men, dwell with them according to knowledge.

Women need men with money. These men need to get some more money -- the right way -- God's way. You would be surprised to find out that a man without a quarter in his pocket wants to know, "Will you marry me?" God has enough money to go around. Men, if you get into the Presence of Almighty God, He will take you from that state of a nickel and a quarter and show you where to go to get work and what to do to have money. You will be what God wants you to be. God wants to make you great, but you must dwell with Him according to knowledge.

In I John 3:22 we see that as we keep His commandments, we get what we ask Him for. You must do those things that are pleasing in His sight. That is why we get what we ask for. There is nothing hard about getting it, for we only need to do that which is right. What a powerful promise! Whatever we are asking for, God will do it because we are keeping His commandments, when we do the things that are pleasing in His sight. When we are obedient, the devil has no place in our lives.

It takes faith to be obedient to God. Faith turns God on; it's like a switch that controls a light. It illuminates God's being. Faith pleases Him. We're all searching for the way to please God and we think that our works are doing it. Wrong! The Bible says that without faith you cannot please Him. In other words, with faith you please God. Without faith, you can't make Him happy. You can't dwell with Him according to knowledge. With faith, you can dwell with God. He's happy and you're happy. You need to believe that He is God, all by Himself. Those who come to Him must believe that He is. Stretch your faith muscles. Believe that He is God and that He can do everything He said He would do. Believe that God is a rewarder of those who diligently seek Him. A rewarder. Think about that. When you diligently seek Him, He rewards you for your search. It's like finding a buried treasure. Because you took the time and effort to finish what you started, you are rewarded with the jewels. You become richer just by the fact that you endured to the end.

Start seeking God in a new way. Seek Him early while He can be found. Find out what God is saying about that day before it ever gets started. Discover where the traps of the devil are located. And remember, the devil shows up when he sniffs out the scent of a blessing.

CHAPTER V

THE WILDERNESS EXPERIENCE

There are many words in our vocabulary to describe the devil, but I think the word "radical" pretty much sums him up! One definition of "radical" in Webster's dictionary is "favoring extreme change." The devil is a changeling and like a chameleon, he is often not consistent in the way he manifests or appears. Often, he tends to do things that you don't really think he would do. He likes to generate talk on the deeds of man: "Did you hear about what he did?" and "Wasn't that something how he did that?"

God wants the world to know that they should also be talking about what the Church is doing. The Church is going to have to get a little more radical-- if we are going to take this world for Jesus. Moreover, the Church has to be very creative and very, very hungry to win the world for Jesus, because every day you try to live saved, the devil tries to talk you out of being saved. Now if he's got the right to try to talk us out of being saved, then we've got the right to talk people into being saved.

Then was Jesus led up of the spirit into the wilderness to be tempted of the Devil. And when he had fasted forty days and

forty nights, he was afterward an hungered. And when the tempter came to him, he said, If thou be the Son of God, command that these stones be made bread. But he answered and said, It is written, Man shall not live by bread alone, but by every word that proceedeth out of the mouth of God. Then the devil taketh him up into the holy city and setteth him on a pinnacle of the temple. And said unto him If thou be the son of God, cast thyself down, for it is written He shall give his angels charge concerning thee, and in their hands they shall bear thee up, lest that anytime thy dash thy foot against a stone. Jesus said unto him , It is written again, thou shall not tempt the Lord, thy God. And the devil taketh him up into an exceeding high mountain and showeth him all the kingdoms of the world and the glory of them;   And said unto him, All these things will I give thee if thou will fall down and worship me. Then Jesus said unto him, Get thee hence, Satan, for it is written thou shall worship the Lord, thy God, and Him only shalt thou serve. Then the devil leaveth him and, behold, angels came and ministered onto him.

Matthew 4:1-11

Here we see Jesus was led of the Spirit into the wilderness. The wilderness represents a place of loneliness and preparation. The wilderness is where God isolates you to take you into a season of preparation for what He has in store for you. Have you ever felt like you were walking alone and wondering where your friends were when you needed them? Wondering where the Church was when you really needed somebody? Have you ever wondered where Jesus really was when you needed Him the most? That's what it feels like being in a wilderness experience. It's like being in a place of dryness where everything is void of moisture; a place where everything around you is dry and you have to figure out how you are going to survive in a setting that is not conducive for your survival. You become like the lone cactus standing erect in the midst of sand and dryness, although there is life in you, you're all prickly and agitated because you can't find another life form anywhere. The writer was right on target when they said, "You've got to walk that lonesome valley and you've got to walk it all alone."

The wilderness is a place of "aloneness." No matter how many other people are in the pew next to you in church on Sunday or in the house with you, you feel as if you are walking a path without companionship. No one seems to understand what you're going through, where you're going, or even how you are getting there.

The world is not fashioned for people that love God to adequately survive. The Bible says we are in the world, but we are not of the world. The Bible also says that if any man loves God, then he would have to be a person who hates the world. He will have to be a person who does not agree with the very things that go against the ways of God. The Bible goes on to say that you are either going to love God or you're going to love the world which is controlled by the devil. You cannot love God and love the world at the same time. You have to love one or the other. Now whichever one you are committed to is the one that is going to control your life. If

I'm committed to God, then God is going to control my life. But if I'm committed to the devil, then the devil is going to control my life. Check to see who has the control in your life.

Out of all the places Jesus could have been, the wilderness seems the least likely. But it was the place of choice. Why was Jesus in this particular location? The Spirit led Him there. He had to be obedient to God to go where His Father wanted Him to go. The key to being in the right place at the right time is by being obedient to God when He tells you where to go. The key to your receiving what you need, when you need it, is responding to God when He says, "Go."

Why was He led there? Simply for the devil to exhaust every bit of authority he had over the life of Jesus; and so that God could show the devil that he's no match for those who are tapped into God.

The key to being victorious is knowing you're going to win before you get started. God already knew that Jesus would be victorious. He already knew the outcome of the situation. There are a lot of us who are currently experiencing things right now and God has already spoken to you concerning the outcome. You're the winner. It's a fact! It is settled in heaven and in earth. But now you must allow this fact to move out of the arena of your mind and move to the arena of your heart. You must know that you know.

Notice, the first thing Jesus did in His wilderness experience was go on a fast. Why a fast? What actually is a fast? A fast is a set time of consecration in which the physical body is afflicted in order to uplift the spirit and soul to a greater height in God. A fast also creates an aroma inside of you, a sensitivity in your heart to hear and ultimately be able to obey God at a higher frequency.

Although there are many types of fasts, Jesus was led to carry out a "total" fast (one with no food or water at all). Jesus gave of Himself totally to God, as a time of consecration and dedication to the service of the Lord. He continued His total fast for the length of forty days and forty nights. Why such an extreme measure? Because Jesus perceived that He would be tempted in the area of His obedience.

> **All the commandments which I command thee this day shall ye observe to do, that ye may live, and multiply, and go in and possess the land which the LORD sware unto your fathers.**
>
> **And thou shalt remember all the way which the LORD thy God led thee these forty years in the wilderness, to humble thee, and to prove thee, to know what was in thine heart, whether thou wouldest keep his commandments, or no.**
>
> **Deuteronomy 8:1-2**

The wilderness is the place that your obedience to God will be tested. That season of testings and trials that come upon you is a handy tool in the hands of God, because He sees just how obedient you will remain to Him. This was a weakness for the children of Israel. They were fine in many other areas but were failing enormously in their obedience to God.

The Scripture above shows us that the wilderness is where our obedience is tested but also gives us the rewards of getting a good grade in this area. Verse one says that when we are obedient, "observe to do", the rewards are that we "may live, and multiply and go in and possess the land." This is good news. I have discovered that my own possession of the land is linked and runs directly proportional to the degree of obedience that I am to my Heavenly Father!

I'll never forget when my brother and I gave our lives to Christ. The church had gone on a fast. The fast started on Monday morning. One of my brothers got up Monday morning and he started off well, He prayed for himself and brushed his teeth and everything. Breakfast was normally around 7:30. I mean, he was really doing well. By 8:30, he jumped up and said, "I can't take it no more!" He started to smell the bacon Mama was cooking and said, "I can't take it no more. I've got to have it." How many of you know that the devil will tempt you when you're doing what God tells you to do? The temptation will not only come in the form of food, but also in money, fornication, etc. The temptation will always be opposite of what God expects.

The devil did not leave Jesus alone while He was in the wilderness. Actually, the devil came to tempt Jesus for several reasons. He came to tempt Him because He was doing what God told Him to do. Now be prepared for this -- whenever you are trying to do right, expect wrong to show up. Let's settle this now. When you decide to start telling the truth, liars will start showing up in your life. When you decide that you are going to commit yourself to your marriage, all of a sudden a whole lot of folks start being attracted to you. Why? Because you're trying to be obedient and the devil is out to try your obedience to God. He wants to disprove your obedience.

The moment you decide that you don't want to put alcohol and drugs into your system anymore, suddenly the enemy will make sure they are available to you freely. As soon as God gives a woman a nice male friend to be nice to her and to respect her, then comes a man who is no good and all of a sudden, he develops a "nice" spirit. As soon as God blesses a man with a respectable young lady that he is interested in and a young lady who respects herself, that old one that just couldn't do right, suddenly gets this "I just have to have you" anointing. All of a sudden something comes over her and she realizes just how attractive you really are, and she also realizes how attractive the one is God gave you. So whenever you're going to do good, bad will show up.

The Bible says Jesus fasted for forty days and forty nights and that afterwards He was hungry. If you're fasting, don't think it's the devil because you are hungry. When you fast and don't eat, you know you are going to be hungry. Hunger is an innate signal that the body needs fuel. Whenever you deprive the body of food for any given time, it will signal you that it is empty by sending the hunger pains. Matthew 4:3 says, "And when the tempter came to him, he said, If thou be the Son of God, command these stones to be made bread."

God has led Jesus into the wilderness to be tempted by the devil. This was God's opportunity to show forth His glory in His Son. He's got Him fasting and here comes the devil to try to make Jesus disobey. The first thing the devil tries to do is to make Him break his fast. He says, "Now, if You're really the Son of God and can work as many miracles as You say, let me see You take these rocks and turn them into bread." Now, why in the world out of all things Satan could have asked Jesus to do, why did he ask Him to turn them into bread? He knew the Man was hungry and that God had Him on a fast. The devil's strategy was to make Jesus disobey God by eating. That is exactly what he did to Eve. Food is potent and has a power to make you lose your focus. Forbidden fruit is not sweet.... so don't eat.

Sometimes, when you are on a fast, someone will say, "I cooked this chicken last night and something told me this morning to bring you a piece." I mean, here come folks that never wanted to take you to lunch, asking "Can I take you to lunch? I'm paying." And you're sitting there, knowing that God has you on a fast, and you let the devil tell you the Lord is speaking to you. Warning! It's a satanic trap! Use your head and tell people, "Thank you, but no, thank you. I'm going to do something else for lunch today." And, you know, people will say, "Aren't you gonna eat? Aren't you hungry?" And you will sit there making up every kind of excuse not to tell them that you don't want to eat that day because you're afraid to tell them you are fasting. You're afraid they won't understand. Rather than telling the truth, you tell them, "I'm going to pick up my car today," or, "I'm going to be doing something else for lunch." Don't go through all that stuff and lie. Don't let the devil make you feel bad about doing what God told you to do. Give God the glory and confess Him before men.

Jesus responded to the devil. You have to be able to talk back to the devil. The devil comes and talks to some of us and we get spiritual. Friends, you'd better speak a language he can understand! When the devil comes to tempt you, that's the wrong time to be talking in tongues. Understand that he doesn't understand that? The Bible says that when we speak in tongues we speak unto God-- not the devil. Speak a language he can understand. Did Jesus start speaking in tongues? NO!!! He answered and said, "It is written, man shall not live by bread alone but by every word that proceeded out of the mouth of God." In other words, "Devil, I'm not going to depend on Myself to make it. I know I'm out here. I'm going through something, but I'm still going to depend on

God." He told the devil, "I don't need food to make it. I'm feeding off of the spiritual food." What did Jesus do? He talked back to the devil, not to Himself.

He didn't throw a pity party and invite all His friends -- anger, gloom, and depression. The devil loves pity parties. Don't party with him. The first time you go through something with your husband or your wife, you think, "he or she doesn't love me." What a lie! You know, it's the devil's job to tell you all that stuff. Jesus said, "I'm going to live by every word that comes out of the mouth of God." I'm not going to pick and choose what I will or will not obey. I'm going to eat everything on My plate, even those things that I dislike because God has given this to Me as My daily bread for this season."

You don't have to let the devil in. You don't have to agree with the devil or allow him to control your life. Make your own decisions. Don't do things that the devil wants you to do. Why walk around full of hatred, when you can have a whole lot of love? Why walk around angry, when you can be glad about what God is doing? Many situations would turn around if we'd stop complaining. "Mary, I'm sick of this job. I'm tired. It's just not doing right." The moment you stop complaining about the job, will be the moment God opens up something else for you. God will not give you anything while you're whining and complaining, crying and whimpering, because if He gives you another job, He's done nothing for you. You haven't learned anything. The Israelites learned many hard lessons due to their murmuring, grumbling and complaining.

Just because you tell the devil "no", doesn't mean he is not going to come back again. Some people get saved and the first time the devil shows up, they get rid of him. He keeps coming back and they think, "I don't know if this Jesus thing is going to work out or not." Of course it is! You must know that in this world, you will be blessed plus persecuted.

Say Deacon X, a good, saved man and full of the Holy Ghost, sees a beautiful woman coming in his direction. The devil tells him, "Would you like to take her out? " Now all of this starts if he allows what he sees with his eyes to get into his mind. The Bible says that if Deacon X looks on a woman that is not his wife to lust after her, he has already committed adultery in his heart. What the devil will do to men in the church, (even men who aren't saved), who are happy, engaged, trying to get married, and trying to do what is right and to live right, the devil will come to mess you up. He says, "Look, what you see with your eyes, don't you want it?"

That is the same question Satan was posing to Jesus. He was using all the material things on the earth to distract Jesus. "I'll offer You all of this. You can have all of this, if You'll just worship me instead." He took Jesus up to the highest point of the city and said, "Now, if You are the Son of God, cast Thyself down, for it is written He shall give His angels charge concerning Thee, and in their hands they shall bear Thee up."

The devil was trying to get Jesus to commit suicide. He said, "If I can get in His mind to get Him to act by what He sees; I can make Him think that this fall is not so far. If He does jump, then the angels will catch Him." Today, the devil is still telling people to take their life. "Kill yourself." Now, Jesus said in St. John 10:10. "For the thief cometh not but for to steal, kill and to destroy. But I have come that they might have life and that more abundantly." Who comes to take your life? And Who comes to give life? Jesus said, "I don't want you to take it, I want you to have it." And the devil is telling people all the time, "Take your life. Take someone else's life." Brothers and sisters, don't think about dying...you've got too much living to do!

First Satan tried to make Jesus eat.. That failed, so now he tried to make Jesus kill Himself. The devil does not always try to make you kill yourself naturally, he tries to make you kill yourself spiritually. He says, "Go ahead and do it. You know it won't hurt you. Just do a little bit. Don't go to church here. Don't participate. Don't be a part of this."

Jesus had to handle the situation without any help. The church mother wasn't there, His pastor wasn't there talking, and the choir wasn't there singing. No one was around to give Him any encouragement, support or anything. Jesus faced the devil one-on-one; He dealt with that rascal alone. If Jesus did it, so can you! Deal with the devil face-to-face.

The Bible says in Matthew 4:5, "Then the devil taketh him into the holy city, setteth him on a pinnacle of the temple." Jesus permitted the devil to show Him what he had to offer. Jesus looked at it and it did not destroy Him. Just because you see something bad with your eyes does not mean it is going to destroy you. Jesus looked on it, the devil showed it to Him, and he tried to enter Jesus' life through what Jesus saw with His eyes. The devil thought, "Certainly, if I let His eyes focus on my power, He will develop an appetite for it. If I can allow His eyes to see, He will develop a taste for it and He'll want it. I could not trap Him with the food issue, so I'm going to try to get into His mind by what He sees with His eyes." How wrong he was! Jesus looked those things straight in the face and turned away from them.

Jesus said, in Matthew 4:7, "It is written again, thou shalt not tempt the Lord thy God." "Listen, devil, let Me tell you something. I know that if I jump, because I am Jesus, the angels will catch Me and take care of Me. But I'm not a fool." In other words, while He knew God could keep Him, He didn't have to prove it to the devil. Just because I know that God takes care of me, does not mean I'm going to get on top of a building and think I'm Superman and dive off. When a person is on drugs they often think they can fly. How many of you know that when you've ingested too much alcohol in your system, you think, "Man, I can whip the whole world?

I'm going to start a fight and turn this party out." That liquor starts talking to you. When you are smoking marijuana, you think you can do things that you really can't. Have you ever been to a party? Sometimes, even the music can make you feel like you can do stuff you can't do. There will be people on the dance floor that can't even dance, but because of what they hear, they think they can do it.

This is why you must be careful what you hear. Your ears are connected to your spirit and what you allow in will affect your spirit and your soul. If you are constantly listening to negative things, you will feel negative about yourself. If you are hearing positive things, you will feel uplifted. Guard your ears.

Many people in the Church are sitting around and waiting for someone else to make them great. Most of the people you expect to make you great never show up! The ones that you think is going to make you successful never comes! Then when they don't show up, you feel like crying. That's bad! Get up and make yourself great! You have to make yourself successful! Stop waiting for other people to bring you happiness. Get up and create your own happiness. "God, send me somebody; everybody else is getting a good husband. Looks like God would give me one." GET UP! Look lovely. Look pretty. Smell good. Make it HARD for a good man to pass you up. Give God something to work with. Smell like a rose. Carry yourself like someone who wants someone to come and get them. Stop crying and dress up!

Wives, if you're tired of your husbands' not spending enough time at home, make your home a place he'll miss every time he's away. Some church women look beat up. Here it is the nineties, and you're dressed in 1920 antiquated styles and colors. Meanwhile, the unsaved women around your husband are dressed in style! Don't you realize that style will help to keep your man's attention?

My wife used to look like that; at twenty-one years old she looked forty. I wouldn't allow her to put on makeup, and she could not wear jewelry. And the Lord knows she had better not think about putting on pants! I learned better! Every man who has a good wife ought to dress her up. If she isn't what you want her to be, keep working with her and be patient. God is not through with her yet!

And brothers, get your stuff together, too! Get your britches off your ankles and put them back on your rear end. Give a lady something to be interested in. When she looks at you and you've got a haircut with 13 arrows going in 13 different directions, she already knows you're confused and so does everyone else! If you can't decide on a direction for your hair, you certainly have no direction for yourself nor can you offer any to a woman. Your image is speaking loudly, "Lady, if you are smart, you will run from me in 13 different directions."

When all else fails, the devil will offer you everything and give you anything just for you to sell out to him. Have you had an ungodly offer lately? Jesus already had everything. That made Him immune to the devil's temptations. To have God is to have everything. Be content in whatever state you are in while you're working to achieve more. Decide that what you don't have will be created by what you do have. Communicate that to the devil. You have to let the devil know that you don't take gifts that have strings attached. The devil tried to buy Jesus and Jesus said, "Your price is too cheap. My salvation costs Me too much. There is no money that can buy this." When the devil comes to you, let him know you are not for sale.

Carry yourself in such a way that everybody knows you don't come cheap. Tell the devil, "You can't have what I paid so much for. It cost me too much and the price is too high." The devil thought, "Surely I've got Him now." Look at what Jesus said. "Look, I'm not going to put up with it, I'm not going to tolerate it. I'm not selling out. I'm not giving up. I'm not trading in My salvation. I'm not trading in what I worked so hard for." Like Jesus, don't sell out. Remember, the price has been paid for you. Jesus paid it, and it's much too high.

Jesus told the devil, "Get behind Me. You have no place in My life. I'm through with you. I'm making it obvious to you that I'm not going to agree with you." The result? The Bible said that after Jesus rebuked the devil, he left! And guess who showed up? The angels of God. There are certain things that you are going to go through and nobody is going to be there until you come out of it. God watched Jesus go through the whole encounter with the devil, and God never showed up to do anything or say anything until the confrontation in the wilderness came to a close. God stayed silent until the matter was settled between Jesus and the devil. God stayed silent until Jesus overcame every temptation.

This is a lesson to learn from Jesus' life. Jesus spoke to the devil and had several conversations with him before He finally told him off. Some days, you can put up with Satan's harassment for a while, but there comes a time when you finally discover that he is trying to destroy you and you must get rid of him. Jesus put up with it for a season, but then He said, "I'm tired of it and I'm getting rid of it." And God showed up. Now the moment that you show God that you intend to go through, He is going to show up and visit you. The moment you prove to Him that you will be obedient at all costs, He comes and ministers unto you. His grace is sufficient to get you through the trial and to the expected end, the blessing of God.

The key to receiving a visitation from God is to show God that you will hold out. You are not going to always have God coming to say, "Hold out, hold out, hold out, hold out, hold out." You must tell God yourself, "I'm holding out, I'm holding out, I'm holding out." You will not always have God showing up to rebuke the devil for you. You have to do it. The devil had Jesus in the right place at the right time under the right circumstances, and he still came up empty handed.

Jesus dealt with his conversations and the devil had every opportunity to make Jesus backslide. But Jesus said, "I will not sell out for anything and anybody. Devil, get behind Me." The Bible said that the angels showed up and ministered to Him. The devil left Him for a season. Why? Because Jesus made it obvious to him that He did not have any intentions of letting Himself get into things which He had no business.

He was determined to be obedient, no matter what. Obedience often means that it will take longer for you to achieve the goal, but in the end it will be worth it. You won't have to lie, steal or kill to achieve greatness and you will be able to maintain success because you know that promotion comes only from God. Do it God's way. Be obedient to the end -- no matter what it takes or no matter how long it takes. In the end, like Jesus, you'll see the angels minister to you the gift God prepared for you. You'll see the enemy defeated, dejected and running away from you because there is no foothold for him in your life.

May God's rich blessings of obedience, forever be your portion.

For a listing of other books and tapes by
Bishop Charles Mellette, write him at:

Christian Provision Ministries
1100 Garden Street
Sanford, NC 27330

(919) 774-9462